Snifting
Baby Jesus

by

Tom Rogers

editor: Peter Roe

w w w . w e s s e x . m e d i a

To Jacqui

My thanks to all who have supported me on this poetic journey. Particularly my friends and colleagues at Apothecary; Ged Duncan, Peter Roe, Tee Francis, Rob Casey. The members of the writers groups Story Traders and Jurrasix Writers.

Very special thanks to Izzy Robertson and Syd Meats for their eagle eyes and gripping hands. ;o)

This collection is not meant as a deep and meaningful autobiographical journey but hopefully will entertain, inspire and challenge none the less

Some of it is true…

Some of it isn't…

"Never let the truth get in the way…"

CONTENTS

Granny Down the Loo

I lost my granny when she fell down the loo
In spite of what everyone told me to do
My sister, my brother, my uncle too
Said "Don't lose your granny when she falls down the loo"

I tried not to lose her but she just slipped away
I said "Granny don't go" I said "Granny please stay"
She said "I am leaving the way of the poo"
I said "Granny that's gross", she said "Boy that's true"

I said "couldn't you go the way of the cow
Munching the cud" she said "Now now
The way of the cow is just to go moo
But I shall slip gently into the loo

Over the ess-bend and into the drain"
I said "As a plan Gran that's more than insane
Couldn't you go the way of the zoo
If you're going that way I'll come along too

There's lions and tigers and elephants OOO"
But a granny must do what a granny must do
So "Stop all your sobbing" she said to me "Hush
You can help me a little, just pull the flush"

Well I looked in her eyes and I said "Granny no
I can't flush you away" I said "Granny don't go"
She solemnly countered "You know what to do…
So I flushed my old granny right down the loo

And then I felt terrible racking my brain
Could I have avoided pulling the chain?
And I looked in her eyes as she slipped down the pan
And she whispered "thanks" and I whispered "Gran"

Then I stood there in silence, what else could I do?
As I watched my old granny descend down the loo

Gurgle…
Gurgle…
Gone.

The Jelly Belly Ballet

The Jelly Belly Ballet
prance and spin and spin and prance
and cause such a din with their marvellous dance
You can hear it from Preston
to just South of Calais

Who is it? The people all ask
causing such a wonderful din
Why?
Comes the reply
It's the Jelly Belly Ballet

Are you out or are you in?
The cognoscenti know what's best
with wobbly thighs, flabby chests
and enormous breasts
Pardon me for noticing
and the grace of a thousand
dainty flying buffalo
No, it's not that infamous *Gruffalo*
It's the Jelly Belly Ballet
Out on tour
If you've never seen them before
You've got something of a treat in store
Always a pleasure never a chore
The Jelly Belly Ballet

The way they shake the earthquake boards
And the audience howl
And roar their applause
You'll know that it's a worthy cause
With flips and double flips
And pirouettes
And double Salamanders
And acrobatic triangles
And a number of thunderous
Dancing pandas
It's the Jelly Belly Ballet

The Jelly Belly Ballet
Don't shilly shally

Or dilly dally
When they're whooping
And swooping
And leaping and loping
And lumping and bumping
All around their reinforced chalet

And they hear the dinner bell go

bong   bong   bong   bong   bong

Then you could hear a pin drop

Plop

Everything must stop

Cos they didn't get where they are today
by not stopping for dinner
They wouldn't be the Jelly Belly Ballet
If they finally got much much thinner
So they must
I'm sure you'll understand
munch   munch   munch munch   munch
Breakfast dinner and lunch
Though not in that order

Then they get back to practising
If you see them it's quite a thing
and you'll

applaud   applaud   applaud

The Jelly Belly Ballet
Masters of magical movement
Only ever verging on wild disorder

Put your hands together for

The Jelly Belly Ballet

Jack and the Beanstalk

"Jack's a no good selfish lad.
He's not like me, he's like his dad"
his mum said over cups of tea
to Florence, Susan, Kate and me
"Meanwhile I slave and grind away
I cook and wash and, come what may
I clean the house and make it 'swell'
but does he notice, does he? Well
of course he doesn't, not a bit
He loafs and lazes like a twit"
"Send him to work, the kid's not dumb"
says me 'n' Flo to Jackie's mum
"He's unemployable by now"
says young Jack's mum to me and Flo
"He's tried his hand at this and that
but always ends up falling flat
'til now he doesn't even try
I can't think of a reason why
and though the cupboards getting bare
he doesn't even seem to care"
Thus it was that when we'd gone
she called the little waster down
and told him "Jack...
The time has come for you to go
out to the market to sell the cow
and though you're but a simple lad
and folks think you're a trifle funny
I'm sure that even you won't find it hard
to sell a cow and make some money"

Jack, who was often verbally battered
put on his coat, all torn and tattered
went to the shed to fetch the cow
"I never liked it anyhow"
he mumbled as he walked away
"What was that Jack boy? What d'ya say?"

"Nothing mother" young Jack said
as he led the heifer from the shed
and went to market where he sold it
and can you believe what he got

the silly clumsy lazy clot?
Three beans, three beans. I think it's tragic
to be graced with a son like that
Of course he says they're magic
well he would, and Doris, that's Jack's mum
sent him upstairs without any supper
then called me on the telephone.
"This time we've really come a cropper"
                she told me
Then blurted out the whole story...
That was a couple of hours ago
and I'd not heard from Doris since
which I thought was a little odd
when out the blue I get this call
from Gladys saying...
"Have you seen this tree?
It looks a little like a bean
It wasn't there a while ago
and Mavis says "you can see it grow"

                So
I looked out the window and there it was
taller than a hat stand, higher than a house
I couldn't believe what I had seen
it was indeed a giant beanstalk

                Wow
Of course they'll have to chop it down
and when they do it'll reach the other end of town
I'll ring the council, really it's a nuisance
You can't grow trees like that without a licence

And then, next morning
there were the folk from the TV
Of course they came around to see
Doris... and Jack, who became a famous gardener
appeared on World in Action and even Panorama
But, do you know, the men from the TV
didn't do a single interview with me
But as for Jack and Doris, well...
They made up all sorts of tall stories
even taller than the bean
about giants and golden eggs and stuff

Honest, I might be green
but for what it's worth
I think they're milking the situation clean
and Doris used to be so down to earth

And have you seen those new age hippy types
bored with crop circles and ancient megaliths?
They make the village look a mess
not that I object to how they dress
but I asked one once
why he just stood and stared all day
He said "This is a cosmic bean OK
a message of peace from another planet"
Then, would you believe, it he told me to can it?
"I'm busy here with vegetable contemplation"
Honest, people like that are just a disgrace to the nation

And when I rang the council up
they said the bean was "of scientific interest
                    had to be protected."
I argued with them, but to no avail,
I told them… "It should never have been erected"

                So
I'm going to chop it down tonight
When all the town is fast asleep
I get a chainsaw, take it out
to where the giant monstrous bean is

and… there's this great commotion
Jack comes hurtling down the beanstalk
                    helter skelter
grabs the chainsaw from me
hacks and hews and chops the beanstalk
which tumbles followed by, no, it can't be
a giant, who lands face down on my cottage roof!

Of course, I shall be asking for compensation

Koala Qabalah

I'm studying the mystical Qabalah
but doubt that it'll do me any good,
I showed the tree of life to my koala
It put him in a very pensive mood
He climbed a Eucalyptus in the garden
Grew sullen, then he made a sudden dash
and now he won't come down til' I beg pardon
For filling up his head with mystic trash
He says "That stuff's medieval, you should bin it"
I told him "it's the roots of modern thought"
"How can it be? There's really nothing in it"
He quipped, then as I searched for some retort
to teach my glib marsupial a lesson
He did a little dance above my head
Which made me laugh because he had a dress on
But all the same I just returned to bed

Then called the pet shop asking for a refund
"My koala's crazy, can I get a cat"
I blurted but the management referred me
to clause 5 of our contract, that was that
"Be warned your koala is sephirothphobic
Remember this and all that it entails
His breath is best when it's not anaerobic
His diets' best when not confined to snails"
The pet shop owner rattled off the clauses
We all ignore when buying a new pet
With relish and a minimum of pauses
Then advised me "you should call the vet
They're perfect if you're looking for a put down"
I told him this approach was quite extreme
But then he just ploughed on, put his foot down
He made the call. We could have been a team

So I felt narked by how the man had acted
But told myself to just roll with his punch
and since the vet would have to drive to get here
I took the time to eat a little lunch
The vet came and debated with my koala
Mocking the way he'd taken to the boughs
"It all depends on phrasing" he assured me
continuing "it even works with cows"
My koala thus descended to the garden
was most forgiving, suddenly at ease
I never speak to him of the Qabalah
but otherwise I just do as I please
Which brings me to the moral of this story
Cos all things have a moral if you look
but only those like these are worth repeating
and binding up and putting in a book
A vet's acerbic comments to koalas
will shame the creatures out of the trees
And if you want to study the Qabalah
remember this, but then do as you please

Blagging

Pardon me for asking
But do you have a biro
I've got to fill this form in
If I want to cash this giro
Got a wife and got four children
And she's always nag-nag-nagging
So I need to get the readies
It's a busy business blagging

It's a busy business blagging
But the bills at home are mounting
And I'd like to hold the job down
But I'm past the age of counting
As a man to climb a ladder
Using corporate connections
And I don't like office politics
Or union elections

Or union elections
So you get to know the bosses
And the bosses try to buy you off
To minimise their losses
Cos you give a Marxist money
And he's suddenly a Tory
And last week how we've got to strike
Is just another story

And it's just another story
That I'm ticking in these boxes
But play the game and fill the form
We must be sly as foxes
'cos the missis needs a boob job
'cos her tits have started sagging
So I need to get the readies
It's a busy business blagging

The Gunpowder Plot

We're nothing on our own
    But here we are piled up
        a black beach in darkness
            Tumbled over each other
                like a universe
                    of atoms
Right out to wooden walls

                that hold us like a cup

Words of death and glory
    Are rumours
        shuttled away from the otherness
           of that barrier
              in every direction

| Bastards | Parliament | Stealing | God |
| Man | Woman | Work | Wine |

So many meaningless words
    We feel the anger
        It's not difficult
           to rage with potential

Each one of us a tiny spark
    If we fell into fire alone
        Like Lucifer on the day of judgement
           it would be a match made in heaven

    W H O O M P H . . .

We can't imagine
    Bricks tumbling over bricks
        or the way that blood
           paints a town red
              better than anything

So If you found these words
    Hidden in our barrel depths
        like a lucky dip at the fair
           Well, that's just you

As it is
        After the dark stillness of waiting
          We feel ourselves
             tumbling over each other
               once again

Red men
Savages
So many meaningless words

Slabs

Grey slabs beneath your feet
Cannot contain their happiness you trod there
Come out all unnecessary
Day-glow effervescence
Loosen their oppressive grip
Over the wild and hidden earth
Give way to grass and daisies

Dead trees regain strength
To bear fruit one more time
Because of the memory of your fingers
On their rough bark
For just a second

Legions of daffodils
Practice yellow trumpets underground
In preparation for a springtime fanfare in your honour

And squadrons, squadrons of market square pigeons
Learn alphabets
So flying celebratory loop-the-loops
They'll write your name in shit
On crumbling day-glow slabs

Sniffing Baby Jesus

The shepherds were sniffing baby Jesus
Passing him round to inhale that odour
of new born infant, talcum powder, love
and freshly crocheted yellow baby grow
Which Joseph, a new man, had dedicated
Evenings to, on the journey, in spite of
The niggling fact it wasn't even his
baby, some white skinned northerner's she said
He'd slipped away after the deed was done
Mary, insensitive as ever called
the git an angel, a flaming angel

It was true he'd always loved her before
but knowing this, let's just say it was a
favour to the parents they'd even wed
Family, friends and all, he couldn't see
them suffer the indignity, so this
happy scene, for which he took no credit
was down to him. The gall of the girl
that she'd questioned his masculinity
moments before the shepherds arrived.
"Shouldn't it be blue" she said. "No, yellow"
he'd assured her, "because it signifies
the risen sun and light and life and he
will be like this for us." But secretly
he doubted this small gesture would succeed
in knitting the family together.
"Yellow crochet. You're such a poof" she'd said

Just then the baby came to him, smelling

He held it to his face and breathed

as the little creature gurgled sweetly.

Shit. It smelt of shit. "Good Lord" said Joseph

pushing the Son of God away from him

"Change a nappy yourself for once in your life"

Joseph was always changing some baby

or other's smelly nappy just to prove

what a thoroughly modern gent he was

So felt quite justified in ending thus

"you spoilt bitch." The shepherds gasped. Embarrassed

Looking at each other like, "Should we leave

now, just make our excuses and you know

Go...."A knock on the door changed everything

"Y E S" yelled Joseph sharply. "What is it now?"

The kings outside, shuffled awkwardly

"The star must have been wrong" said Balthazar

quietly "Come on, let's go for a curry"

But as Jesus hung there crying, stinking

and thrust away from the sour faced Joseph

dangling in his grip, Mary swung the door open

"How lovely of you gentlemen to come"

She beamed. "Pay no attention to sourpuss

over there, he's having one of his turns"

The Complete List of the Damned
(the book of death is more economical than the book of life)

You're damned if you do

And you're damned if you don't

And you're damned if you didn't or you did

You're damned if you know it

And you're damned if you show it

And you're damned if you keep it all hid

And you're damned if you think that you're not damned

And you're damned if you think that you are

And you're damned if you closed every door to the damned

And you're damned if you left one ajar

You'll be damned if you left any open

If you did then you'll never get far

You're damned if you drive

You'll be damned if you survive

You'd be damned in a bus or a car

You'll be damned if you think that you're walking

You'll be damned if you're fixing to swim

You'll be damned by the tide

And the fact that you've tried

You'll be damned if you're left on a limb

And you're damned if you try to be normal

And you're damned if you think you're a star

You'll be damned with your throttle in the bottom of a bottle

You'll be damned if you drink in a bar

You'll be damned if you hold down a good job

You'll be damned if you work for the man

You'll be damned if you can't or you are or you aren't

And you're definitely damned if you can

And you're damned if you sign your name on a line

And you're damned if you're looking for work

You'll be damned by the monks and the priests and the punks

And the soldiers and the filing clerks

So you're damned if you're slick

Or you're born with a dick

And you're definitely damned with breasts

You're damned if you're quick

Or pretend to be thick

And you're damned if you fail any tests

And you're damned if you think that you're not damned

And you're damned if you're not very sure

Of the categories I missed

On the bottom of this list

You can whistle if you want any more

Ornaments

Don't give me ornaments and stuff
it's just a waste of time
I'll only hang my coat on them
or cover them with slime
from half a pot of mouldy jam
I do it all the time
I filled that lovely jug you gave
with Rizla, brushes, biros
The Gainsborough's a pin-board for
receipts from last year's giros
The Ming vase near the pile of coats
I keep bus tickets in
The other of the pair I broke
whilst pissed on smart price gin
There's paint on all the furniture
and dust beneath the tables
and pages of old magazines
are pinned to Tudor gables
But as for what you'll find beneath
the cushions of my sofa
I found these eggs marked Fabergé
and the stuffed corpse of a gopher
A present from my uncle Bill
the taxidermist preacher
It really was quite generous
but not for the poor creature
Although I take part of the blame
I shot it with my rifle
an antique from the civil war
its muzzle's full of trifle
So as you see these objets d'art
I've looked after them well
Give me another one this year
and I'll send that to Hell

The Fart in My Air

You're the fart in my air
    The nits in my hair
    The broken bar
        in my cage full of bears
    The liquid tar
        in my ocean of tears
    The poisoned tip
        to my enemies' spears

You're the crack in my dam
    The scab in my jam
    The green in my ham
    My Chernobyl lamb
You're everything   I do not like
The piss in the tank of my super-bike
You're generic lager in a real ale pub
    Second rate ketchup on top notch grub
    The bucket that Dad used to drown trapped mice
  In short   you're not very nice

You're the small seed of doubt in a bill of good health
    The mountain of debt in a mirage of wealth
    The dream of a tumour on iron lungs
    A promising keeper corrupted by bungs
    The weeds in my flowers
    The waste of my hours
    The ghost of twin towers
    You're wedding day showers

You're everything   I do not rate
The fly in my ointment, the crack in my plate

You're the hope of a nation invested in lies
    A serial killer's alibis
    The plumber's excuse
        the unflushable poo

So it's hardly surprising
    a.)   I love you   b.)   I hate you
    c.)   I've grown quite fond of you over the years
        So much so that I feel quite lost without you.
    d.)   [*choose your own ending*]

TV Utopia

There's people who have loved and lost, the same's not true for me
I never loved, so never lost, I sat and watched TV
There's people who for years fight wars, defending liberty
I find my freedom here indoors gazing at my TV
There's BBC and Channel 4 and even ITV
With digital there's so much more for everyone to see
A hundred thousand channels beam around our heads it seems
I'd like to keep on adding more, these televisual dreams
Might put an end to hate and war, we'd stay at home instead
and watch a little telly before we went to bed
We wouldn't have to eat too much. Without much exercise
our food bills could be cut in half. Our index finger sizes
'd probably increase a bit from flicking through the channels
whilst practicing remote control skills, 'til we land on panels
of contestants for a quiz show from the comfort of our sofas
We'd hang around and learn a bit like uber telly loafers
Now criminals could clear the streets in search of entertainment
and prison service guards could give up seeking their containment
The burglar'd stop burgling, the rapist stay indoors
The murderer would drop his axe to hear the grand applause
that comes with sit-com happiness on channel forty three
Now coppers, seeing crime had been consigned to history
would hang around the station watching reruns of The Bill
while scientists at last discover "telly cures the ill"
which leaves no need for doctors, nurses, surgeons and the like
I haven't yet quite figured what'll happen to this mic
but soldiers'll stop fighting when they see the telly schedule
and astronauts won't bother climbing on that lunar-module
and the men who make decisions in the corridors of power
will find that no one's listening, besides, "cometh the hour
cometh the programme". Cricket should keep those bastards glued
Besides, what isn't listened to is seldom misconstrued
Now religion could go quietly to channel forty seven

The pope'd give up praying'n' go straight to telly heaven
where he'd meet the Dalai-Llama for the great TV debate
with Buddha, Ghandi, Jesus and The Devil, who'd be late
and they'd all get on famously like famous people do
until the ratings saw them moved to late night channel two
and that'd leave a vacancy for television God
which might be Richard Branson or that Rupert Murdoch bod
But no matter who our saints are and whichever gods we choose
we'll always have the telly so humanity can't lose
Yes
We'll always have the telly so humanity can't lose
Yes
We'll always….B e e e e e e e e e e eep
We apologise for the disruption to this programme
This is due to factors beyond our control
Normal service will resume as soon as possible.

Rural Fashion Tips
(Stuck on the horns of a dilemma?)

Be wary of the scary cows
Observe the anger on their brows
Allow such space as time allows
Avoiding any bovine rows

Do not give in to Jersey wiles
Nor Guernsey batted eyes and smiles
The Friesian flatters you for miles
Whilst guiding you away from stiles

Such scary cows can read your mind
Be wary of them or you'll find
They'll chew the cud, seem quite kind
Before they charge you, rob you blind

Rainforest Economics

The notion you can save a world
from melting ice caps, rising seas
is difficult to grapple with
if you're engaged in felling trees

that regulate the CO_2
and oxygen, but then again
what is a man supposed to do
to raise himself when better men

can't feed their kids or treat their wives
when money's tight and work's so sparse
If you think mine should go without
to save your world then kiss my arse

The only work round here is this.
Be moral and you'll waste away
It's best that we don't understand
what armed policemen tend to say

concerning crops we grow instead
of this earth's lungs. She'll grow some more
and western fools will buy the coke
that keeps our kids from being poor

and US planes will fly the stash
we need since they destroyed our land
to hyped-up radicals in bars
who speak of living hand in hand

with all world, a happy bunch,
while snorting lines in public loos
then wandering off back to lunch
discussing songs about the blues

with advertising sales execs
who live a life of blessed ease
and think that you can save the world
by telling us to spare the trees

Poetic Tourettes

I've got poetic fucking Tourettes
I can't help but swear and curse
but unlike with ordinary arse Tourettes
I do it in bollox verse

It was my mum who noticed it first
she said "fuck I don't mind if you rhyme
but every shit wank bum you say
d'you have to swear each time"

Well fuck I went to the doctor
to see what the clit could do
"He said bollox arse fuck twat
I can see what's wrong with you

You've got poetic fucking Tourettes
You can't help but swear and curse
but unlike with shit wank bum Tourettes
you do it in bell end verse"

Now I find it a bit annoying
'cos I can't keep an arse crack job
when I answer the phone with fuck you sir
and I end with tit wank gob

and there's no new deal on benefits
when they say you're tosser rude
so what's a man like cunt fuck me
supposed to do for food

Cos I've got poetic fucking Tourettes
I can't help but swear and curse
but unlike with shit wank bum Tourettes
I do it in cunting verse

Yes I've got poetic fucking Tourettes
I can't help but swear and curse
Arse crack bollox fuck twat balls
and it's cunt flap getting worse

Arse crack

and it's cunt flap getting worse

Barry Evans' Mum

I haven't got a thing to say
which means I'm keeping schtum
about what happened yesterday
with Barry Evans' Mum

And gentlemen don't kiss n' tell
so I won't breathe a word
about what happened yesterday
unless perhaps you heard

The bumping through the ceiling
and the creaking of the springs
and Barry Evans' Mother
when she orgasms she sings

And there was lots of singing
in Barry Evans' house
but being sworn to secrecy
I'm quieter than a mouse

About what happened yesterday
with Barry Evans Mum
but speaking off the record
I can make a woman cum

in fifty different sharps n' flats
although I wouldn't bother
citing this in reference
to Barry Evans Mother

My Foot

My foot has fed my teeth with toes
when I was two or three

Suffering no nonsense
your foot is put down easily
On this
And that:
Snail shells, problematic arguments, difficult emotions
It splats the lot

My foot
on the other hand
is sometimes stuck up
like a rich bloke's nose

Like it went to public school

and thinks itself above the usual push and shove
Hovering
a bird of prey
say

Or its' bunioned and hammer-toed self
bound up as a China girls'

easily broken

Suspended in some technological contraption
Weeks on end

You might suppose
my foot has a stick up its arse
and consequently walks a little funny
But

One day my foot went fucking crazy
First one foot then the other
Left right left right left right left
Like they were a team or something
A platoon
Right into the ocean

Superfly

The fly's a spy I tell you
The ants out in the garden
all file away with messages
to give to Scotland yard 'n'
probably the CIA
the FB blinking I
Chief of all these insects
is known as Superfly
and Superfly is dangerous
he bugs you when you speak
He monitors your visitors
the secrets that they leak
Don't think he didn't notice
the day you picked your nose
  hen Mrs Eldritch left the room
  iow everybody knows
  'hugs inside the government
  iave sent a swat team out
  n case the snot's Al-Qaeda snot
they come to flush it out
and that's who all these ants are
with their nudge-nudge biscuit crumbs
disguising hi-tech weapons
small grenades and micro guns
They rush up nasal passages
the moment that you sleep
to look for terrorists in there
before they softly creep
down cheeks with petri dishes
packed with samples of your bogy
which they send beneath the pavement
to a beetle with a stogie
and a microscope
who takes a while
when solemnly confirms
"Your greenies have been tampered with
by evil axis worms"
The Ladybirds have seen 'em
in the garden near the roses

so buy yourself a fly whisk
'n' always blow your noses
cos they'll send in the mosquitos
even if you're just a patsy
they'll start a propaganda war
they'll say that you're a Nazi
they'll Photoshop the pictures
from the spider's hidden camera
and no one will believe ya'
and journalists will slam ya'
when they see how you've conspired
with the woodlouse on the step
to blow up bloody parliament
or some malicious schlep
And they'll say the world is cleaner
when you're whisked off in the night
but then perhaps they'll see it
as it crawls around the light
The Superfly has just moved in
spies on a different subject
One day it will be you
so learn to fight the insects
and always sweep the kitchen step
and always spray the roses
and always burn your handkerchiefs
after you blow your noses

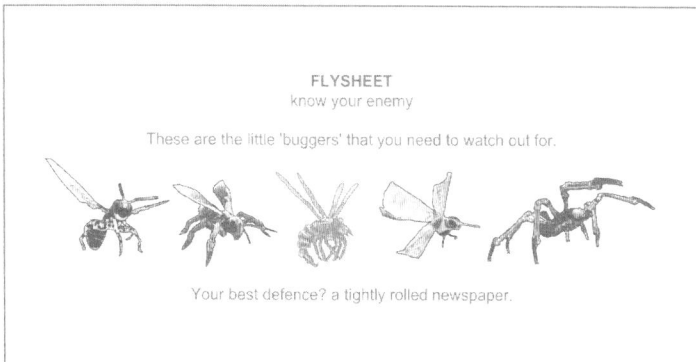

FLYSHEET
know your enemy

These are the little 'buggers' that you need to watch out for.

Your best defence? a tightly rolled newspaper.